THE AMAZING DINOSAURS

A Coloring Book

P.A. SCHOONOVER

Gotham Books
30 N Gould St.
Ste. 20820, Sheridan, WY 82801
https://gothambooksinc.com/

Phone: 1 (307) 464-7800

© 2022 Pat Schoonover. All rights reserved.

No part of this book may be reproduced, stored in a retrieval system, or transmitted by any means without the written permission of the author.

Published by Gotham Books (August 12, 2022)

ISBN: 979-8-88775-006-4 (sc)
ISBN: 979-8-88775-007-1 (e)

Because of the dynamic nature of the Internet, any web addresses or links contained in this book may have changed since publication and may no longer be valid.

The views expressed in this work are solely those of the author and do not necessarily reflect the views of the publisher, and the publisher hereby disclaims any responsibility for them.

Introduction

A huge variety of dinosaurs ruled the earth for millions of years. Some fed on plants and lived in large herds, while others were fearsome meat eaters that hunted other dinosaurs. They could be as big as the 30 ton Brontosaurus or as small as the tiny bird like Archaeopteryx.

Dinosaurs lived from the Late Triassic Period, through the Jurassic Period, until the end of the Cretaceous Period. No one knows why they mysteriously died out about 65 million years ago, but there are a lot of theories.

Can you find mother Dinosaur's hidden eggs?

Hot To Trot

Who's Your Daddy?

Can you guess my name?
(my name means Roof Lizard)

True Love, Big Time

My name means Horned lizard Who am I?

My name means Tyrant lizard king
Who am I?

Can you say Leaellynasaura?

LEE-el-in-a-SAW-ra

Did you know?

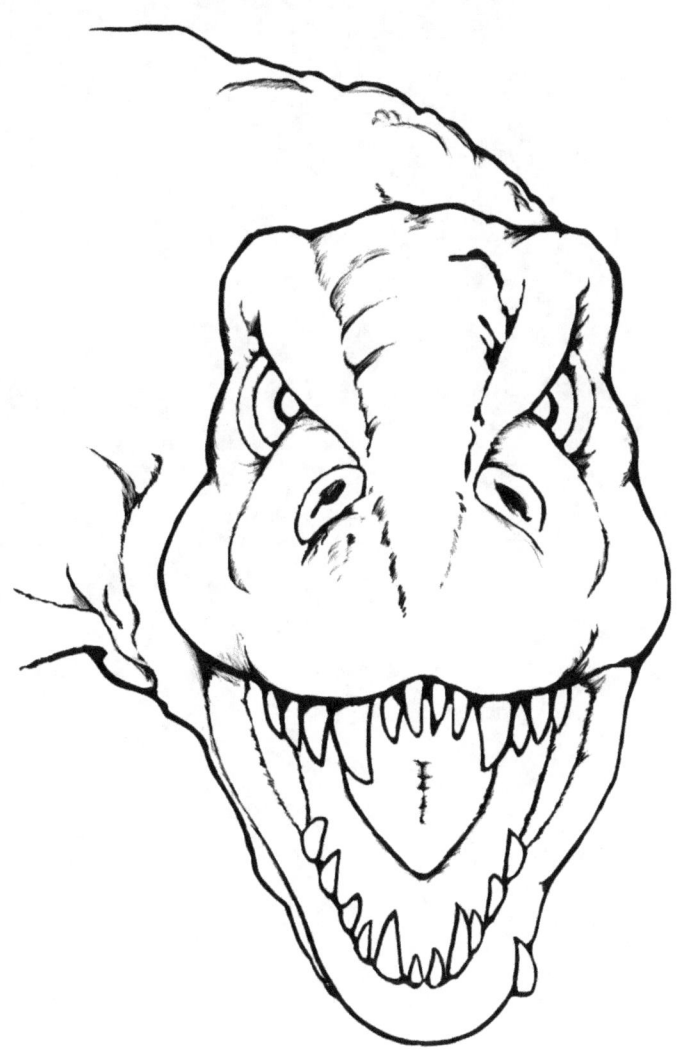

Tyrannosaurus Rex was one of the largest flesh eating animals to have roamed the earth?

Did you know
Deinosuchus
DINE-oh-SOOK-us

was an immense crocodile, that could have been 50 ft. long?

Draw Me!
use the grid as a guide, and draw Triceratops.

Did you know Styracosaurus stih-RAK-uh-SAWR-us was a plant eater?

Cryptocleidus lived in shallow seas, and was a fish eater

Archaeopteryx
AR-kee-OP-ter-ix

lived in tress, had feathers and ate bugs!

Answer Page
Page 7. There are 9 eggs
Page 13. Stegosaurus
Page 17. Ceratosaurus
Page 19. Tyrannosaurus

www.ingramcontent.com/pod-product-compliance
Lightning Source LLC
LaVergne TN
LVHW062001070526
838199LV00060B/4229